The Writings of
Ron Baratono

The Writings of Ron Baratono

Ron Baratono

ISBN: 1508634335
ISBN 13: 9781508634331

Special Thanks:

I would like to thank you, dear Lord, for how all my words came to be. I'm forever grateful for your blessings. I would also like to give a special thanks to my personal friend and editor, Becky Capps. She gave me tremendous guidance during the process of writing my book. Last, thank you all for reading. God bless you. In Jesus's name, amen.

Table of Contents

Family Reflections

It was 8:00 a.m.; the year was 1962. I was in my grandmother's living room, and I remember standing at the picture window. When I saw my father walking down the driveway, I had a strange feeling. I think it was anxiety. It made me cry. When my father disappeared in the fog, the anxiety grew stronger. It's strange that I can remember anxiety at three years old.

I saw the taillights go on at the stop sign, four houses down, and the feelings returned. Somebody lifted me off the floor and brought me to the room down the hall. The door closed; the thump echoed in the small bedroom. I ran to the door and pulled on the handle with all my strength. I was crying. I could feel the heat of frustration on my face. Repetitious bangs echoed in the room as I kicked the bottom of the thin wooden door.

Suddenly a spell of exhaustion brought me to my knees. There I lay, slowly falling asleep. In the distance, I could still hear my mother crying. When I think back, it was as if I had woken up in another bedroom.

Flash forward to when I was five; only a couple of years had passed, but life wasn't the same. Somebody changed my last name, and I had a hard time pronouncing it. There was a baby in a crib that constantly cried and two other children I wasn't familiar with. It felt like we had just met. I can remember wondering when I was going home. The days turned into years; all started to seem the norm. There was a splendor about the house, a comfort and charm to my new room.

There were two little girls, my sisters. Their hair was dark brown, and their eyes were almost black. Our father's complexion, like that of the little girls, was an olive tone. His hair was black and wavy, combed straight back. His eyes were dark brown and his nose a little too big for his face. His forearms were hairy and large; they stuck out of the short-sleeve dress shirts he always wore.

Anthony, my dad, stood six feet four inches tall. My neck would get sore trying to ask Dad a question. It was so relieving when he would finally pick me up off the floor.

"What do you want, son?" he'd ask. His voice was a deep baritone. I always knew he wasn't my real father; I never cared. It was only the violated feeling of being abandoned I despised.

Even as the years passed and I grew into a young man, the feeling of being betrayed stayed in my mind. How could someone just leave me? I thought, "What's wrong with me?" Those were questions I asked myself as a boy. It wasn't long before I discovered that there wasn't anything wrong with me, yet I still shoved the question "Why?" deep into the back of my mind.

It was because of my adopted father that values, a sense of security, and self-esteem were embedded in my nature. He taught us that order came first. I remember his powerful hand on my rear end when I knew I had it coming. His deep voice put the fear of God in us kids, but we never questioned his love.

He taught us the most important ethic in life: love your family, something my biological father never did. Now here I am, thirty years later, with two children of my own. Who knows what life would have been if this experience hadn't happened. But because it did, I'm a much better person. Because of this wonderful new father and the insight he gave me, I'm the loving father I was meant to be.

Those adolescent years were the happiest years of my life. They taught me the real ethics of life—a balance, a steady medium, and a real ideal that were met in the end with wisdom. The truly important things in life are our children. Through all of this, I can stand and feel I'm repaying my society by living up to my obligations as a father. I hope my children can feel what I'm teaching them.

Last summer I finally met my biological father. I was walking out of the liquor store; the sun was hot—it beat down on the blacktop parking lot as I made my way to my car. There was a man sitting in an old Chrysler next to me, his windows rolled down. The car was covered with rust; only a slice of burgundy showed on its hood.

I was opening my car door when the man yelled for me to come over. I thought it was strange that he knew my name. I walked over slowly and stood at his car window. I asked him what he wanted. He stepped out of his car and grabbed me around the neck. He was crying.

I could feel his tears on my bare shoulders. Right at that moment, I realized who he was. I could smell the whiskey on his breath. There I stood after he let go of me, my mouth dry, my mind blank. He looked little and old, his face swelled from the alcohol. I was staring into my own eyes, but his eyes told a story. They had a glare. They were searching for another drink. It took all of three minutes for him to ask me if he could borrow two dollars. I gave him the money, and he said that he loved me and that he had known he would find me.

I didn't have the nerve to tell him he was the one who was lost. It was then I wanted out of the situation. I said good-bye, and I walked away from his car. It was the longest walk of my life. I wasn't going to let myself cry. Even after twenty-nine years, the feelings of not being wanted returned.

On that day, I left the past behind and discovered a new insight about myself. I felt like a king in my own heart. Russell Kirk said, "It is the spirit, the spark of Godhood, which raises Man above all the rest of creation and makes him distinct in kind from all other living things." It's wonderful to know who you are.[1]

---

1. Pico Della Mirandola and Russell Kirk, *Oration on the Dignity of Man* (Washington DC: Gateway Editions, 1996), XIV.

My Life

Disappointments that I face
and the mountains that I climb,
the valleys that I cross—
a journey in time.

The heartbreak that I felt
and the happiness I steal
have led to this day
where everything is real.

I might cross a thousand miles
and fall along the way,
but everything I've learned
has brought me to this day.

Being me without question,
being me without doubt,
loving everything around me—
That's what life is all about.

Sharing Jesus
A tribute to my friend Mari Stewart

There was an image on the cross
and the meaning of his words—
things I didn't know at all,
yet my purpose still was heard.

My heart seemed always empty,
fulfillment not in sight,
down the empty path of wonder
and where to turn in life.

On a summer day a friend stopped by;
she taught me how to pray.
The Holy Spirit filled my heart
and now lives with me each day.

The meaning of his words are clear,
and his image shines so bright;
the purpose of my heart's so real—
Jesus Christ has changed my life.

Dear Jesus

Thank you for the words I write
and for your guiding light,
for the grace you show
and the love I know.

For the words I speak
and the love I seek,
the ties that bind
and this love of mine.

For the grace you give
and the life I live,
your light that shines
in this heart of mine.

The Storm

The storm that you woke up with
that's rolling in your head,
it's all the things we keep
inside before we go to bed.

We can't swim across the ocean
and we can't row against the tide,
but every storm has beauty if we
dare to look inside.

Imagine for a minute of
how happy life would be
if we focused on the future
as far as we could see.

Dark Clouds

Among the clouds I found God's grace
when the silence was too loud,
when things in my heart got heavy,
I lay there without a sound.

I found the greatest things in life
are not about the clouds;
it's not about the rain that falls
or the silence that's too loud.

When things in life get heavy
and the roads are hard to bear,
it's in that moment of God's grace
we know he's standing there.

Empty Room

When life's like an empty room
that's burning deep inside, and
thoughts of how things used to be
seem so far behind.

In our hearts we hold God's grace
that's there to show the way,
opening up brand-new doors
that help us out today.

An empty room has meaning;
it's free of any doubt.
It's a wonderful new beginning,
and that's what life's about.

God's Strength

The light in your heart's not weakness;
the kindness you give is for real;
the love that God gives you can cherish;
it's all in the way that you feel.

Spending our lives with his meaning,
reaching for things with his grace,
sharing our joys with each other,
and keeping our hearts in one place.

The strength that God gives is forever;
all weakness and doubt will be gone;
our lives are filled with his meaning;
forever we will be strong.

God's Hands

Dear God, I reach my hands to you,
and I pray for an inner calm.
So the many things that bother me
will somehow all be gone.

Dear Father, I need your grace again.
Please pick me up once more,
and take me to that peaceful place
you blessed me at before.

It's a place in my mind
that only you can understand;
as I reach into the heavens,
I can feel you touch my hand.

God's Gift

I woke up to another gift today.
It's life for me to live,
another day of happiness
and another day to give.

I'll follow my dreams of happiness
and follow my dreams of love,
looking to God's graciousness
that's sent from up above.

Thank you, Father, for another chance
to love with all my heart.
Today your gift of happiness
gives me a brand-new start.

Start with God

Do you carry too much on your shoulders
and carry too much in your heart?
Do the burdens of life lie beside you,
and you're worried there's no place to start?

Does your purpose in life seem to escape you?
Are you wondering which way to turn?
When you look at your life, if you question,
then maybe there's more you can learn.

Placing your worries with God's meaning
and holding him next to your heart,
you'll find all your beginnings aren't empty,
and this is the best place to start.

Thank You, Mom

No matter how old I get,
you make me feel young.
I guess it's because you've been there
since before my life had begun.

Thank you for your guidance,
your patience, and your love.
Through all the days of happiness,
God sent you from above.

There's nothing like a mother's love
that fills my heart this way.
I love you, Mom, so very much and
happy Mother's Day.

God's Path

A look back on the path you took
is filled with such regret.
Do your feelings follow loneliness
or a fear of discontent?

Yesterday is gone,
and, you've learned along the way,
it's the path of being wiser
and that's what's here to stay.

God led you to new places.
He knows what you went through.
That path you took, he held you up—
it's what you had to do.

Through the winding roads of life,
you'll find a narrow turn;
it's God's way of showing us
there's more for us to learn.

Remembering Love

Remembering loved ones in a wonderful way
as they pass through the light of the day.
They move to the Lord in heaven above,
and we think of them with lots of love.

It's in God's hands that we trust and love;
and we know that his light above
is the calming strength we lean on here.
In our hearts they are always near.

My Sadness

Sadness is a part of life
some people never see;
they look at me, and I'll smile back—
that's how I'm supposed to be.

I hide my tears through sunshine
and hide them through the rain,
hoping that these people
will never see the pain.

These endless thoughts of sadness
lie heavy on my mind;
I look upon my faith, dear God,
to help me all the time.

The part of me that's empty,
you fill with so much love;
my faith has brought me peace, dear God,
sent from up above.

God's Straightened Path

The stages of the life I live—
at times so out of place—
the path I'm taking seems so nice,
but it's only for God's grace.

It's only for the love of God
I walk without a care;
the road I travel might be long
but not so hard to bear.

I lean on God throughout the paths
and smile along the way,
acknowledging his love for me—
I know he's here to stay.

My tattered thoughts are puzzling,
at times so out of place;
I trust in God's direction
for a straightened path of grace.

Blessings in Disguise

Today there was a piece of life
that was somehow out of place—
a missing touch or quiet smile
in a cold and empty space.

Sometimes we go through changes
that are hard to understand;
then we lift our hands to God above
and let him know we can.

The tests of life aren't easy;
sometimes they bring us down.
It's only with our faith in God
that we finally come around.

We realize that the piece of life
that once felt out of place
was a blessing in disguise
in a different time and space.

The Joy in God

Sometimes our worlds come crashing down
with nowhere else to turn—
a broken heart, or loneliness,
our bridges left to burn.

In God we have a special love
that's there to see us through;
a joyous kind of hope in life
made just for me and you.

We took him in our hearts one day;
we know the reason why.
It's in the times of hardship
that he's there to get us by.

We all need extra strength in God
through good times and the bad—
his special kind of joy in life
that helps us when we're sad.

My Tears in a Bottle

My tears could fill a bottle
with broken dreams of love,
recorded in my memory,
sent flying like a dove.

Looking to the heavens
for God to show the way;
strength and love, my happiness,
I live for him each day.

He recorded all my sorrows,
kept track of all my tears,
the book of empty promises
and a book of all my fears.

Today the dove flew back to me
with a note from God above;
the note was in that bottle
and filled with so much love.

The Depth of Our Hearts

There are times our hearts grow cold
as we wander through the night,
searching for some happiness
while darkness fills our lives.

With every single step we take,
we come closer to the Lord,
sifting through life's promises
in search of something more.

The depths of our hearts shine bright
when we kneel down and pray.
It's a newfound understanding—
we can live for God each day.

When searching for true happiness,
it's our hearts that find God's grace,
hope, love, and blessings,
in a bright and peaceful place.

Stronger Love

When things in your life get broken
and your heart is on the mend,
you just don't know which way to turn,
and it's hard to try again.

But God will never leave your side—
His love is yours to keep.
When searching for which way to turn,
there's no mountain that's to steep.

He understands what you're going through,
your fear to try again;
in God we have a stronger love
that's there until the end.

Don't Be Afraid to Love

Don't be afraid to love
when the tears come pouring down;
when everything feels hard to you,
God knows you'll come around.

Feelings of uncertainty,
self-doubt, and all its strife,
God will make you wiser
every day of your life.

Open up your heart to him;
there's a reason for your tears.
It's a way to make you stronger
and to wash away your fears.

Our Journeys

The rich man who said he was hungry
and the poor man with a smile,
they danced around heaven's gate
but only for a while.

When heaven's gate was opened,
they both came walking in—
the poor man with his smile
and the rich man with a grin.

They both knelt in front of God
as he listened to them pray;
in front, the fruits of happiness
brought on one golden tray.

Our journeys are often different,
but in the end they are the same—
our love and search for happiness,
all in Jesus's name.

Winds of Time

As the winds go rushing by,
so do our lives and time;
there will be days of loneliness
that lie heavy on our minds.

But looking to the Lord,
we find joy in every day;
our own special place in life—
it's nice to live that way.

As those winds go rushing by
and the years go by so fast,
in God we have a special love;
it's one that always lasts.

Quiet Emptiness

Thoughts of quiet emptiness
and the reasons why we're here
lie silent in our minds
and the things that we hold dear.

There's freedom that's deep inside;
no matter if there's pain
or years of broken promises,
life is not the same.

God has changed so many things,
and in the silence of our minds
we find a greater meaning
that's with us all the time.

Christmas Gift

Holidays can be a lonely time
while your Christmas tree shines bright—
the colors of unhappiness
and the colors of your life.

The glitter fades away from you
as you pretend to hold it near,
searching for a reason to smile
and looking for some cheer.

Underneath the tree of lights
lies a gift he gives to you;
this gift of many blessings
is the gift that's always true.

In God we have a special gift
among lights of green and gold;
Christ the Savior is our gift—
it's the gift we always hold.

Judgment

With judgment all around us,
we look into the crowd;
what's said won't change a single thing,
but the words you hear are loud.

The hearts of insecurity,
reckless voices coming through—
do you have a little more than they
or is it something they can't do?

In God we have such peace of mind;
his voice won't be so loud.
God's words are all that matter
as he sits above the crowd.

Happy Birthday, Jesus

Where would we be without our faith
and the day that we were born?
Our quest for everlasting life
is love and so much more.

You've shaped our lives with hope,
taken care of all our needs—
a life of endless happiness
and a world where we believe.

New Year's Heart

Open up your heart today
to a sweet and silent cheer
and a place you've never been before
where everything is clear.

There's part of you with faith inside
just waiting to come out;
there's never been a better time
to learn what it's all about.

The grace God gives is yours to keep;
it will help you make your way—
the silent cheer deep in your heart
and a happy New Year's Day

Broken Pieces

God's blessed me many times;
it's hard to feel the pain,
the yesterdays of anger,
and days it always rained.

All the broken pieces
that fell onto the floor
were put back together
even better than before.

Rolling with life's changes—
that's what we have to do.
No matter how hard it seems,
it's God who always knew.

For all the broken pieces
God placed upon the shelf,
he blessed me in so many ways—
they seemed to fix themselves.

Unstuck

There's your past that surrounds you
when looking at your life—
the pain that you hold inside,
lost feelings of delight.

Don't measure new beginnings
from a narrow, bumpy road.
Our lives are filled with ups and downs;
it's God's love that you can hold.

Step away from the past today,
and look at how you've grown—
a brand-new piece of heaven
that you can call your own.

Her Broken Heart

Through the loveliness of her face,
you'll find a broken heart;
somewhere on the path of life,
her world was torn apart.

The sadness that she holds inside,
through a smile, her heart pleads,
wishing to be held so tight—
the fulfillment that she needs.

What happened to this lonely heart
that reaches for your hand?
Will you be the wonderful man
who tries to understand?

Healing Heart

Looking for the things that hurt
or the pain you felt for sure,
bringing those thoughts into your life,
is more pain that you'll endure.

Tomorrow's just a breath away
and the moments that you love;
toss away an angry heart,
and reach for God above.

There's a purpose for every memory,
through the pages that you live;
find your place in happiness
and a reason why you give.

Patience of the Heart

How vast the space of emptiness!
It's our lives that change with time,
holding on to God so tight,
afraid to be left behind.

Waiting for a change of pace,
missing pieces in your mind,
the empty hole that's dug so deep—
that loneliness inside.

Patience for the special gift,
the love we crave so dear,
until that day they come to us—
it's God who's always here.

Golden Dreams

There's a suitcase full of golden dreams,
turned rusty after time
when set upon a broken bed,
left waiting in your mind.

The need to forget the past
will never go away,
until you look within yourself
and start a brand-new day.

The day you take those rusty thoughts
and wash them from your mind,
you'll see that all your golden dreams
will find a way to shine.

Love Is Gone

Essence of the love is gone;
like a winter chill, it passed,
fading from my memory—
it was never meant to last.

The efforts of forsaken dreams
lie naked in my heart;
through frozen tears of emptiness,
I'll find a place to start.

The winter chill won't last for long;
it's the strength you gave to me.
I'm so much stronger now you're gone,
and that's what's meant to be.

Hey, Girl

Don't think so deeply, girl;
there are always changing times.
God is way ahead of us,
not only in our minds.

Hey, girl, you do the best you can
in a world not always fair;
through the deepest parts of your heart,
there's a man who will always care.

A broken heart will always pass;
it's our faith that gets us through.
There's a bright and very certain time
that God has planned for you.

The Quiet Horn

Blow your horn so quietly,
while you listen to them speak.
They'll turn away from unwanted tones
before they kiss your cheek.

There will be the wise ones
who care less about the crowd,
who do their work for passion
and never speak too loud.

The horn that blows on a quiet night
down the alley of your dreams
is a silent horn of happiness,
what your passion truly means.

Yours Forever

Look at us under a thousand stars,
and you'll find the day we met—
the blessing of a lifetime
and the day we won't forget.

Today's just a reminder,
like the thousand stars above:
I'll be yours forever
with a never-ending love.

Happy Valentine's Day

As Children Gaze

The eyes of children see so much
that's new with their first chance
to look at life so peacefully,
measuring love with just a glance.

The pieces of our lives we give;
with a smile, we hide our tears—
this lifetime job of worry
and a future full of fears.

They're smarter than we think they are
as they gaze upon our hearts;
a reflection of God's guiding grace
is the place where they can start.

Their souls are always searching,
staring steady with their eyes;
they'll reach for life's true meaning
in the way we live our lives.

Mirror of Fears

This fear of a lifetime
is resting on your face;
it's your own self-depravation
that you have put into place.

Shadows of mistaken thoughts
that line your inner soul;
you carry with you every day
the ones you always hold.

Wash away the pending fear
that you have put in place;
start today and love yourself—
it'll be resting on your face.

The Light in Your Heart

What do we want out of life
when stuck in the same old routine?
The light in your heart has gone dim,
wondering what life really means.

You search for hope in the darkness,
then look for that someone to hold;
treading the days with no answer,
this stage of your life has grown old.

Hanging on to God so tightly,
though life seems so shattered and torn;
someday my heart will shine brightly—
the answers will all be reborn.

Forgotten Words

It was many years ago, he gave my life away.
My dad didn't have the time for me;
he didn't want to stay.
There were more important things
that took his heart away.

The years went by so quickly,
and I turned into a man;
even as a young adult,
he never took my hand.

He never told me why he left that summer day
or if I'd done something wrong or why he couldn't stay;
as a child I searched my heart, looking for his love.
I felt defeated most the time, not knowing God above.

The years kept flying by, I heard he passed away;
stopping by the funeral home, I sat outside to pray.
Knowing I wouldn't hear the words I had searched for all
my life,
I'm still here to visit him through all the pain and strife.

This is the man I've become with children of my own,
raising them with a loving heart even while they're grown.
Touching his hands and walking away, my search is
finally through;
rest in peace and guide my way—that's all I ask of you.

My Life Today

Disappointments that I faced
and the mountains that I climbed,
the valleys that I crossed—
a journey in time.

The heartbreak that I felt
and the happiness I steal
have led to this day,
where everything is real.

I might cross a thousand miles
and fall along the way,
but everything I've learned
has brought me to this day.

Trusting God without question,
loving him without doubt,
praising Jesus all day long—
that's what life's about.

Ron's Quotes and Prayers

Dear God, I'm afraid of the things that I don't understand. I'm even afraid of you, God. Please open my heart to your love. Show me how to understand and how to live with you each day. I don't want to look weak, God, but the truth is I am weak because I don't know you at all. Please come into my heart and allow me to push aside my pride and accept you totally into my life. Thank you for saving me. In Jesus's name, I pray, amen.

Dear God, I ask that today and every day that follows you wash any anger from my heart. I desperately want to look at the world differently. Please help me understand that this anger is hurting me more than anyone else. Teach me to find love in every situation and then to find peace in my heart for the rest of my life. In Jesus's name, amen.

True peace of mind is calm in your heart that you can't explain.

Dear God, I don't ask that my life be perfect but that you allow the myriad of emotions in my life to end each day with calmness. May I sleep peacefully to do your work again by morning light. I ask for these things in Jesus's name, amen.

The appreciation of your success will only come with your perseverance.

We tend not to look at the bigger picture of our lives and instead dwell on the small things that irritate us. When we focus on the bigger picture, those small things fade away.

May today find you happiness and a calm in your heart from God you can't explain.

Goodness follows goodness, all in God's time.

Constant thoughts of money, possession, and control are a personal prison. Thoughts of God, family, and happiness are freedom.

Freedom of the mind is the most important liberty we have. Our belief in God's grace gives us that freedom.

Dear God, let me find calm in every situation. Let me look at others with pity instead of anger. Let me pray they make it through life's fog they've created for themselves and find you. In Jesus's name, amen.

Discrimination weakens the soul and the strength of a nation.

Unkind acts are like giving a piece of one's self away for cheap.

Our own random acts of kindness allow us to receive a gift each day in our hearts.

Dear Lord, I ask that you help me make it through today with patience, understanding, and calmness in my heart. I ask that you replace any darkness in my life with light and my frustrations with joy. I ask these things in Jesus's name, amen.

Attention serves a person better when he or she works for it and then lets it come.

When people judge they completely lose sight of the blessings on their own tables. Jealousy or conviction is a very dark room.

It only takes one sentence to change someone's life. Make it count.

Each day is a blessing, and I awake wondering what wonderful thing, no matter how big or small, will happen to me today.

Dear God, I don't ask for fame and fortune but for an opportunity to embrace many. I don't ask you to make my life perfect but full of love. With every mistake I make, or with any success I have, I ask to feel your grace along the way, for the rest of my life. In Jesus's name, amen.

You're not going to always hit a home run in life. You're going to strike out! You're going to walk to the dugout of life, frustrated, while spectators chirp your name in judgment. They're afraid to even get on the field, and you know it. The fact that you get back up there, unafraid, going after that next home run, makes you the person you are.

Dear God, I ask that you help me with the darkness I've been feeling and that you help me make today a changing day in my life. I ask you, dear God, for calm in my mind and your light in my heart. I ask these things in Jesus's name, amen.

The whole world would be much happier if everyone was just average.

Love your haters; they're the ones who are really paying attention to you.

People are never going to act exactly like we want them to. So if we stop expecting things from others, we'll find peace in our hearts that will last a lifetime.

Pretending I'm all grown-up seems like too much work. I'd rather just be me; it's effortless and much more fun.

It's best to have a small boat of friends where everyone rows than an ark of friends where no one does. At least you're getting somewhere.

There's calm in the mind of the humble. An unmistakable peace of not having to prove anything to anyone.

When we look and feel happy, it's beautiful and more attractive than anything we could possibly imagine.

If we occupy our minds with self-loathing or negative thoughts, then maybe we don't have enough to do.

When we face every challenge with optimism and learn to fail with our heads up, a great attitude is always success, no matter the outcome.

Our self-worth is not who we know or what we know. Our self-worth is in what we do.

If we think about each other's feelings, then we're never alone.

If we are wonderful parents and family members, then there's really nothing else to prove.

A woman's smile will always make a good man's day.

We all reach a point in our lives where time is the most expensive thing we have.

Worrying about things that haven't happened yet is like riding on the hood of your car—what's the point?

When you surround yourself with wonderful, productive people, you become enhanced. Your level of happiness increases, which is your success.

God brings wonderful people into our lives. He also takes people out to protect us from harm. When we roll with God's grace, we feel his wisdom.

When we first wake up every morning, there's a calm in our minds. The challenge is to keep it there all day.

Being in a bad relationship is like trying to dance when you're sad.

Sometimes God takes people out of our lives for a period of time. Sometimes we need to adjust, appreciate, and reach an understanding of just how important they were to us. And sometimes it's right at that moment when God brings them back in our heart.

I think we spend more time thinking of things to deal with than just letting them go. When we quiet our minds, that's true freedom.

The greatest musicians never cared to be rock stars. They just wanted to play. The greatest actors never cared to be movie stars; they just loved their craft. The greatest artists painted on canvas to fill their own hearts. It's how we truly feel about things in life that will determine our success.

Our journey without judgment can begin today.

People spend way too much time with hatred, jealousy, and drama when kindness is so easy. Grab ahold of the good things in life; they'll take you to places you've never been.

The greatest person to know in life is yourself. There's no one who will treat you better.

The greatest accomplishments in life come from the heart.

The truly important people in our lives are always in our future.

Your true character in life is your destiny.

When I look at your smile, I can see your heart. When I look at your heart, it makes me smile back.

We will never find the perfect job, relationship, or situation. What we can do is search for happiness. Our ideals in life are set by others, and it's because they haven't mastered the art of the happiness search.

The reason a lot of people can't find happiness is because they don't look for it. They allow themselves to be stuck in the same situations. Sometimes happiness comes with the courage to break free.

Never adjust your day to suit someone else's happiness. When riding on God's good grace, roll with things your way.

As we get better at knowing God's love, we grow into better things that surround our lives.

There will always be a part of your life that's not quite in order. This is the growth part, the area where lessons come from. Embrace this! Learn from it, and then move on.

The right path in life will always come with patience. It's when we reach an understanding that everything happens in God's time that we walk the right path.

Dear God, please take the stains off my heart. If there's even an ounce of pain I feel that someone caused me in the past, I ask that you wash it away. Give me strength, show me forgiveness is the healthiest option for me, and set me free. I pray you give me peace today and every day, allowing me to totally leave my past behind. In Jesus's name, I pray, amen.

Biography

Ronald David Baratono was born in Detroit, Michigan, and is the second of four children. From 1984 to 1985, Ron directed *The Blarney Stone Show* broadcast on Wayne Cable Television. From 1985 to 1990, Ron often performed community and dinner theater in Michigan.

Ron hired into the Auto Co. in 1977 at the age of eighteen, where he worked for thirty years. During that time, he still followed his passion for writing and acting. Ron studied at Northwood University and received his bachelor of business administration in 1995 while working full time.

He is the author of the personal nonfictional short story "Family Reflections" and of poems such as "My Life," "Dear Jesus," "The Storm," "Dark Clouds," "God's Strength," and "My Sadness." In addition, he has quotes that are read worldwide.

Ron is also a dad, which he considers the most rewarding job there is. He is the proud father of two wonderful adult young men, who are the highlights of his life. Ron retired from the Auto Co. in 2007 at the age of forty-eight. Today, he continues to follow his passion for writing and acting, appearing in numerous films, including Disney's *Oz the Great and Powerful.*

Made in the USA
Middletown, DE
03 July 2015